MY EMERGENCY

FUSION

EPILEPTIC SEIZURE

By Charis Mather

BEARPORT
PUBLISHING

Minneapolis, Minnesota

Photo Credits:
Images are courtesy of Shutterstock.com.
With thanks to Getty Images, Thinkstock Photo, and iStockphoto.

Front cover – Achiichiii, Deman, azmanq, Anna_leni, elenabsl. 4–5 – Irina Strelnikova, sirastock, Svitlana Bezuhlova. 6–7 – Sudowoodo, aShatilov. 8–9 – HQuality, Agnieszka Marcinska, New Africa, Tverdokhlib, fizkes, Marian Fil. 10–11 – tomeqs, Anastasia Klevakova. 12–13 – Roquillo Tebar, sokolenok. 14–15 – VanReeel, ladybirdstudio, NotionPic, wavebreakmedia, Roquillo Tebar. 16–17 – vystekimages, Cristian Zamfir, Roman Samborskyi. 18–19 – Asier Romero, TY Lim, fizkes, Arsenii Palivoda, Russamee, ziggy_mars. 20–21 – wavebreakmedia, SewCream, Jovanovic Dejan. 22–23 – SergiyN, Juice Flair, YanLev, EvgeniiAnd, Dmitry Lobanov.

Library of Congress Cataloging-in-Publication Data is available at www.loc.gov or upon request from the publisher.

ISBN: 978-1-63691-970-6 (hardcover)
ISBN: 978-1-63691-975-1 (paperback)
ISBN: 978-1-63691-980-5 (ebook)

For more information, write to Bearport Publishing, 5357 Penn Avenue South, Minneapolis, MN 55419.
Printed in the United States of America.

CONTENTS

Would You Know What to Do? 4

What Is Epilepsy? 6

Feeling an Aura 8

Epileptic Seizures 10

What Happens during a Seizure? 12

What Can You Do? 14

Getting Help 16

Triggers 18

How You Might Feel 20

What Next? 22

Living with Epilepsy 23

Glossary 24

Index 24

WOULD YOU KNOW WHAT TO DO?

Let's learn what to do in an emergency. This is when something **dangerous** happens. What can we do if someone needs help?

Would you know what to do in an emergency?

Some people have something called epilepsy. They can need help very suddenly. By learning more, we can keep our friends safe.

WHAT IS EPILEPSY?

Your brain tells your body what to do. It sends messages all the time. But sometimes a brain with epilepsy sends signals it should not.

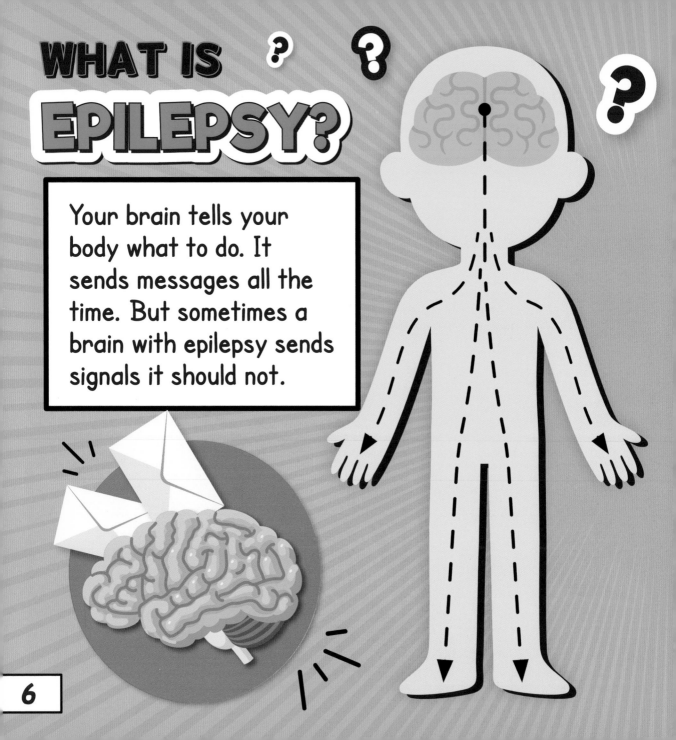

When the wrong signals are sent, it can make someone lose control of their body. This is called a seizure (SEE-zhur).

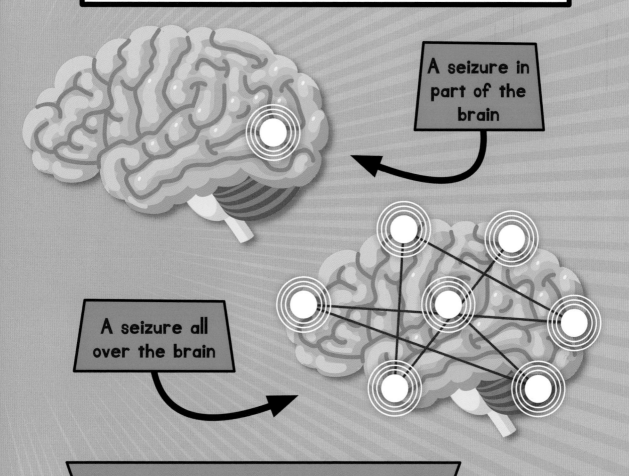

A seizure in part of the brain

A seizure all over the brain

A seizure can affect just part of the brain or the whole thing.

FEELING AN AURA

Sometimes, people with epilepsy get a feeling that they are about to have a big seizure. This feeling is called an aura.

An aura is also called a **focal** seizure.

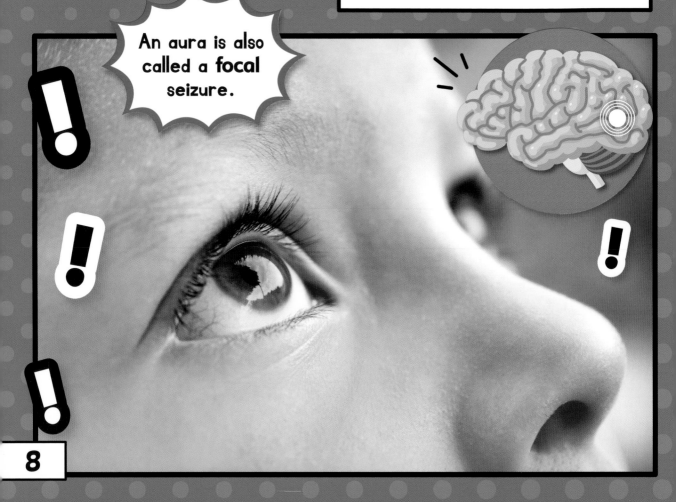

What might happen to someone having an aura?

Their tummy might feel strange.

They could taste, smell, or see something odd.

Their arm might not move normally.

They could suddenly feel happy or scared.

They might get a **tingly** feeling.

An aura is a mini seizure in a small part of the brain.

EPILEPTIC SEIZURES

Not all seizures look the same. Another kind of focal seizure can make someone move in **random** ways. They might . . .

Walk around

Rub their hands

Pull at their clothes

Look like they are chewing

During this type of seizure, the person will not be able to pay attention to anyone else. It might look like they are sleepwalking.

It can take some time before a seizure ends.

WHAT HAPPENS DURING A SEIZURE?

A person can have other kinds of seizures, too. A **generalized** seizure affects all of their brain. It can make their body move in unusual ways.

Sometimes, someone's arms and neck might twitch.

Another type of generalized seizure can make someone with epilepsy fall down. When this seizure happens, they might start shaking and twitching.

Falling during a seizure can be dangerous if the person hits their head.

WHAT CAN YOU DO?

When someone has an epileptic seizure, it is important that we do not do anything that will hurt them or us.

DO NOT

Try to move the person

Put anything in their mouth

Hold them down

15

GETTING HELP

Someone at 911 can help you if there are no grown-ups around. Ask a grown-up to show you how to call 911 so you know what to do during an emergency.

Many people with epilepsy do not need help from 911 during small seizures.

If you need to call 911, they will ask you some questions.

What is your emergency?

My friend is having a seizure.

We will send help. Where are you?

Elm Road Elementary School.

It is important to call 911 only during emergencies.

TRIGGERS

Nobody knows what causes epilepsy. But there are some things that can make seizures happen more often. These are called triggers.

What are some triggers?

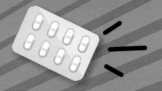

Not taking epilepsy **medicine**

Not getting enough sleep

Feeling stressed

Seeing flashing lights

Not eating regularly

HOW YOU MIGHT FEEL

It can be upsetting to see someone have a seizure. But try your best to stay calm.

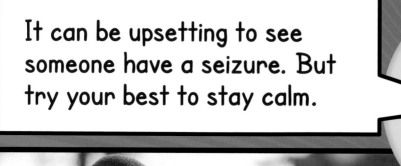

If you are upset or worried, talk about it with a grown-up.

Even if we are scared when someone has an epileptic seizure, we should always treat other people kindly. Seizures can be scary for people with epilepsy, too.

WHAT NEXT?

People with epilepsy have to be careful when they do certain things, such as . . .

Riding a bike

Climbing up high

Going swimming

Taking a bath

LIVING WITH EPILEPSY

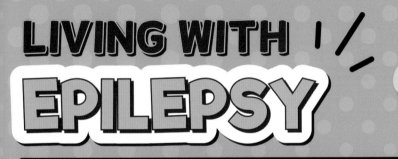

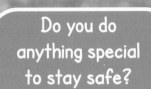

Do you do anything special to stay safe?

I take medicine from my doctor. It stops most of my seizures. It also helps if I sleep well.

Always do what your doctor tells you.

GLOSSARY

dangerous involving possible harm

focal affecting one small area

generalized affecting a wide area

medicine something used or taken to fight off sicknesses or pain

random happening in a way that is different than expected

tingly a strange numb or buzzing feeling

twitch to make a sudden, unplanned movement

INDEX

arms 9, 12
auras 8–9
bodies 6–7, 12
brains 6–7, 9, 12
doctors 23
grown-ups 5–16, 20
heads 13, 15
lights 19
911 15–17
triggers 18–19